DATE DUE

Great Artists

Marc Chagall

ABDO
Publishing Company

Joanne Mattern

visit us at
www.abdopub.com

Published by ABDO Publishing Company, 4940 Viking Drive, Edina, Minnesota 55435.
Copyright © 2005 by Abdo Consulting Group, Inc. International copyrights reserved in all
countries. No part of this book may be reproduced in any form without written permission from
the publisher. The Checkerboard Library™ is a trademark and logo of ABDO Publishing
Company.

Printed in the United States.

Cover Photo: Getty Images
Interior Photos: Art Institute of Chicago p. 29; Art Resource pp. 11, 13, 17; Bridgeman Art Library
     pp. 15, 25; Chagall Archives pp. 9, 12, 14, 16; Corbis pp. 19, 21, 23; George Mitrevski
     p. 26; Getty Images pp. 1, 5, 27

Series Coordinator: Megan Murphy
Editors: Megan M. Gunderson, Stephanie Hedlund, Megan Murphy
Cover Design: Neil Klinepier
Interior Design: Dave Bullen

Library of Congress Cataloging-in-Publication Data

Mattern, Joanne, 1963-
   Marc Chagall / Joanne Mattern.
       p. cm. -- (Great artists)
   Includes index.
   ISBN 1-59197-841-6
   1. Chagall, Marc, 1887---Juvenile literature. 2. Artists--Russia (Federation)--
Biography--Juvenile literature. I. Title.

N6999.C46M43 2005
759.7--dc22
   [B]
                                                                2004052803

Contents

Marc Chagall

Marc Chagall is considered one of the masters of modern art. His paintings are full of symbolism. He used various mediums to create his artwork, including etchings and stained-glass windows.

Chagall was born in Russia. His family was Jewish. So, Jewish and Russian folktales were an important part of Chagall's paintings. When Chagall was a young man, he left Russia to live in Paris, France. There, he further developed his distinct painting style.

Chagall had a lively imagination. He enjoyed combining the figures of animals and people in his paintings. Sometimes, the people floated right off the ground! Chagall's artwork used odd shapes and rich colors to show a dreamy, magical world.

Chagall lived to be 97 years old. During his long life, the art world changed in many ways. However, Chagall's paintings were always full of poetic, colorful images. They stayed true to his vision of the world.

Marc Chagall

Timeline

1887 ~ Marc Chagall was born on July 7 in Vitebsk, Russia.

1908 ~ Chagall painted *The Dead Man*.

1911 ~ Chagall painted *I and the Village*.

1912 ~ Chagall painted *Self-Portrait with Seven Fingers*.

1915 ~ On July 25, Marc and Bella were married. Their daughter, Ida, was born one year later.

1923 ~ Chagall was asked to illustrate *Dead Souls*. Later, he also created etchings for a book of fables and for the Bible.

1942 ~ *Aleko* premiered in Mexico City. Chagall designed the costumes and scenery for this Russian ballet.

1943 ~ Chagall painted *The Juggler*.

1944 ~ Chagall's wife, Bella, died. Chagall stopped painting for nine months.

1960 to 1962 ~ Chagall designed windows for a hospital in Jerusalem.

1973 ~ On July 7, Chagall had a museum dedicated to him.

1985 ~ On March 28, Chagall died.

Fun Facts

- Today, Vitebsk is in Belarus on the Asian continent. This area was once part of the Soviet Union.

- According to Marc Chagall's autobiography, he developed a stutter in the Russian-speaking public school he attended. Chagall explained his stutter as a response to the pressure he felt as a Jew in a primarily Russian school.

- St. Petersburg became Petrograd in 1914. Then, it was called Leningrad from 1924 to 1991. With the fall of the Soviet Union, the name was changed to St. Petersburg once again.

- Moyshe Segal was Chagall's Yiddish name when he was born. He changed his name shortly after he arrived in Paris in 1910, so it wouldn't be so obvious that he was Jewish.

- In 1997, Chagall's home in Vitebsk became a museum.

Life in Vitebsk

Marc Chagall was born in Vitebsk, Russia, on July 7, 1887. He was the oldest of eight children in the Chagall family. Marc's father was named Zahar. His mother's name was Feiga-Ita.

Marc's family did not have a lot of money. His parents worked hard to provide for their children. Zahar was a laborer in a herring warehouse. Feiga-Ita took care of the family's house and the children. She also ran a small grocery store to bring in more money.

Marc's hometown of Vitebsk was in western Russia on the Dvina River. About 65,000 people lived there. Vitebsk was an important port city and railroad stop. Many businesses and factories crowded the city's streets.

Like many people in Vitebsk, the Chagalls were Hasidic Jews. They spoke Yiddish. Religious traditions were an important part of their life. So, Marc grew up believing that God was present in everyone and everything around him.

The Chagall family in the early 1900s. From left, back row: Marc, sister Zina, Uncle Neuch, and sisters Lisa and Maria. Front row: sisters Anna and Maroussia, parents Feiga-Ita and Zahar, and sister Rosa.

School Days

Marc went to a school called a heder, which is a Jewish elementary school. There, Marc learned **Hebrew**. He also learned about Jewish stories and traditions from a **rabbi**. His days at the heder were fun and interesting.

When Marc was 13, his mother registered him in public school. The teachers and students only spoke Russian. Marc did not know Russian. When the teacher called on him, Marc could not say the answers.

The language barrier was not Marc's only problem at school. The only subject he did well in was **geometry**. He preferred to do more creative things, such as singing or playing the violin. Instead of paying attention in class, he often looked out the window and daydreamed.

Marc daydreamed about what kind of job he wanted. He knew he did not want to be a laborer like his father. He thought maybe he would be a musician. He also liked to dance and write poetry. However, none of these were things he wanted to do for a lifetime.

Rabbi of Vitebsk *was completed in 1914. The influence of Chagall's Jewish heritage is seen in many of his paintings.*

Young Artist

One day in school, Marc saw one of his classmates copying a picture out of a magazine. Marc could not believe his eyes. He did not know that people could do that. Marc quickly borrowed a magazine from the library. He took it home and copied a picture from it.

Marc discovered he loved to draw. He was good at it, too. Marc copied many pictures. He hung them up on the walls of his bedroom. Suddenly, Marc knew exactly what he wanted to do. He told his mother and father he wanted to paint.

Chagall in 1906

Animals were an important part of the Jewish and Russian folktales Chagall heard growing up. These paintings of The Rooster *were completed at two very different times in Chagall's life.*

Marc's parents could not understand why he wanted to be an artist. Feiga-Ita tried to convince him to become a clerk instead. However, she saw he had talent and wanted him to be happy. She was able to convince Zahar to let Marc take art lessons.

Art Lessons

In 1906, Marc began taking art lessons from Yehuda Pen. Pen was a Jewish artist who ran a school of painting and drawing in Vitebsk. When the Chagalls couldn't afford Marc's lessons anymore, Pen taught him for free.

While not considered a great artist, Pen was known for his paintings of Jewish life. This may have influenced Marc to paint so many scenes of Vitebsk throughout his career. As Pen's student, Marc would walk around the city and paint pictures of the Jewish houses and narrow streets.

Marc met other young artists while at art school. He soon became friends with a young man named Victor Meckler. One day, Victor suggested that he and Marc go to St. Petersburg, Russia.

Yehuda Pen

Vitebsk is the subject of many of Chagall's paintings.
He usually painted it as a quaint village, as in Over Vitebsk.

At first, Marc was not excited about going to St. Petersburg. He did not want to leave his family. He did not know how he would make a living in a large city. However, Marc knew he could learn a lot about painting in St. Petersburg. He decided to go.

In St. Petersburg, Chagall had a difficult time finding a place to live. For a while, he did not even have enough money to eat well. He eventually got a job working for a photographer.

Chagall also had difficulty getting into an art school. As a Jew, he could not attend the famous arts academy in St. Petersburg. He also failed the entrance exam to another art school.

Chagall ended up studying at the Imperial Society for the Protection of Fine Arts. But, he was not satisfied with his schooling there. He received a lot of **criticism** for his work, and he left soon after. He painted *The Dead Man* in 1908. The fiddler on the roof is a common image in Chagall's work.

Leon Baskt

Chagall eventually began studying under Leon Baskt. At that time, Baskt was a master of theater design in Russia. Chagall was influenced by Baskt's use of rich colors and his interest in folk art.

Chagall eventually met a rich, Jewish lawyer who gave him money and a place to live. Because of this patron, Chagall was able to keep studying and painting. During a visit to Vitebsk in 1909, he met a young woman named Bella Rosenfeld. He and Bella quickly fell in love.

The Dead Man

Self-Portrait

Chagall stayed in St. Petersburg for three years. In 1910, he moved to Paris, France. At that time, Paris was the center of the art world. Chagall began to feel like he had two homes, Russia and France.

In Paris, Chagall attended several art schools. But, his true education came from visiting Paris's many art museums. Seeing what other artists had done helped Chagall experiment with his own style of painting.

Some art **critics** say Chagall did his best work in Paris. His paintings were not as serious as the ones he had created in Russia. Now, his artwork was filled with bright colors and flying people. In 1911, Chagall painted *I and the Village*.

Scenes of life in Vitebsk dominated much of his work. One year later, Chagall painted a picture called *Self-Portrait with Seven Fingers*. In the painting, he is drawing a scene from Vitebsk. Paris can be seen through a window.

Artist's Corner

Marc Chagall

One of Chagall's key works from his first years in Paris is *I and the Village*. Though early in his career, his distinct style was already developing.

Chagall was known for repeating images in his artwork, such as flower and animal symbols. The bright colors and upside-down people are also common elements in his paintings.

I and the Village is an example of how Chagall's memories influenced his art. Viewers can see Russian peasants and Vitebsk. The green face on the right is probably Chagall himself. The images create a magical, dreamlike world. They seem to float across the canvas.

I and the Village

Revolution

Chagall's art was gaining notoriety. He exhibited his work in the annual Salon des Independants and Salon d'Automne in Paris. In 1914, an art dealer invited Chagall to show his paintings in Berlin, Germany. The show was a huge success.

Next, Chagall went back to Russia to visit Bella and his family. **World War I** began in 1914, and traveling was not safe. So, Chagall stayed in Vitebsk and painted. On July 25, 1915, Marc and Bella were married. A year later, their daughter Ida was born.

In 1917, the **Russian Revolution** began. The Russian people overthrew the monarchy and formed a new **communist** government. Chagall was very enthusiastic about this change for his homeland.

Soon after the revolution, Chagall helped organize an art school and museum in Vitebsk. He worked hard. However, the communists did not appreciate his artistic style. They didn't see how it related to the revolution. Chagall eventually resigned from his position at the school.

In 1915, Chagall painted a picture of himself and Bella called **Birthday**. *He felt that he loved her so much that he wanted to fly.*

In 1920, Chagall moved to Moscow, the capital city of Russia. There, he designed sets and costumes for the Jewish State Theater. He had learned this art while studying with Baskt. Two years later, Chagall decided to leave Russia for good.

Modern Master

Chagall moved to Berlin. There, he learned engraving. Then in 1923, Marc, Bella, and Ida moved to Paris. Upon arrival, Chagall found that the paintings he left there before the war had disappeared. So, he started creating new versions of these works.

That same year, Chagall met a man named Ambroise Vollard. Vollard owned an art gallery and was hiring artists to illustrate books. Vollard asked Chagall to create etchings for the book *Dead Souls* by the Russian writer Nikolay Gogol.

Dead Souls launched Chagall's career as a printmaker. Over the next few years, he did many lithographs and etchings. He also continued to paint gouaches and some large canvases. His paintings were filled with flowers and lovers.

Chagall was now a famous artist. Some of his most well-known works from this time are *Green Violinist* and *The Circus*. He had his first American exhibition in 1926.

After **World War I**, Chagall and his family traveled often. He went to Palestine in 1931 to prepare etchings illustrating the Bible. Between 1932 and 1937, Chagall also visited Holland, Spain, Poland, and Italy.

Many of Chagall's paintings are centered around flowers. Here is a painting called **Bouquet Illuminating the Sky.**

Art Terms

Here are some words that will expand your knowledge about art:

engravings ~ figures, letters, or designs cut into a surface.

etching ~ the art of printing from an engraved metal plate to produce pictures or designs.

gouache ~ a type of painting that mixes watercolors with a kind of gum. This creates a shiny, textured surface on the canvas.

lithography ~ the process of printing from a smooth stone or metal plate. The surface of the image soaks up the ink, while the blank area around the image repels the ink.

medium ~ a mode of artistic expression or communication.

modern art ~ painting, sculpture, architecture, and graphic arts from the 1900s and the later part of the 1800s.

A Dark Time

On September 1, 1939, **World War II** began. In June 1940, Germany invaded France. The German leader Adolf Hitler was forcing Jews into **concentration camps**. Chagall knew that it was not safe for him to stay in France.

The Museum of Modern Art invited the Chagalls to visit the United States. The family arrived in New York City in 1941. Chagall was impressed with the size and energy of the city.

Chagall's first important job in North America was to design the scenery and costumes for a ballet called *Aleko*. The ballet was based on a Russian story. It premiered in Mexico City, Mexico, in 1942.

Chagall painted some of his best-known works in the United States. One was *The Juggler*, which he created in 1943. In late August 1944, Bella suddenly became very sick. One week later, she died.

Chagall was heartbroken. "Everything is darkness," he later wrote. He did not paint at all for nine months. Then in 1945, he was offered a job he couldn't refuse.

The Juggler

A New Life

In 1945, Chagall was asked to design the scenery and costumes for another ballet. It was Igor Stravinsky's *The Firebird*. He said yes, and began working again. The ballet and Chagall's designs were a great success.

Chagall was soon busy with other projects as well. He started painting again. The next year, the Museum of Modern Art arranged a huge exhibition of his work.

By this time, Ida was a young woman. Now that her mother had died, she thought her father might be lonely. She suggested that Chagall get a housekeeper.

Ida hired a woman named Virginia Haggard McNeil. Virginia had a young daughter named Jean. Soon, Marc and Virginia fell in love. In 1946, they had a son named David.

A backcloth from Stravinsky's ballet, **The Firebird**

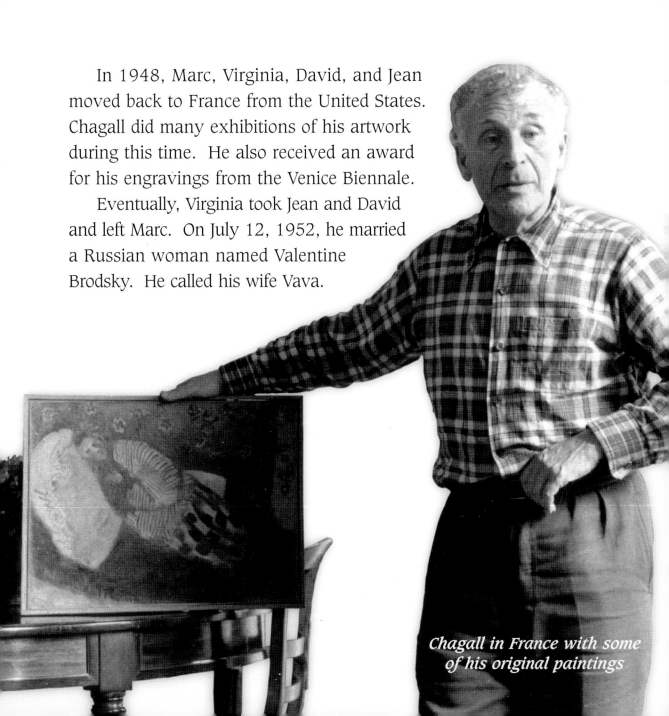

In 1948, Marc, Virginia, David, and Jean moved back to France from the United States. Chagall did many exhibitions of his artwork during this time. He also received an award for his engravings from the Venice Biennale.

Eventually, Virginia took Jean and David and left Marc. On July 12, 1952, he married a Russian woman named Valentine Brodsky. He called his wife Vava.

Chagall in France with some of his original paintings

Painter of Light

In 1957, Chagall began using a new medium. He created two small, stained-glass windows for a church in France. Chagall thought this was the perfect kind of art because the windows were filled with light and color.

Between 1960 and 1962, Chagall created 12 stained-glass windows for a hospital in Jerusalem. He also designed *The America Windows*. This project was created to celebrate the 200th birthday of the United States.

Chagall continued to work on theater design, too. He completed projects for the Paris Opera and the New York Metropolitan Opera.

France honored Chagall by building a museum to display his work. The museum opened on July 7, 1973. This was Chagall's 86th birthday. At that time, it was the only museum in France that honored a living artist.

Chagall continued to paint, even when he was very old. He died in Vence, France, on March 28, 1985. The world still remembers him as a great artist who filled his work with imagination, magic, and color.

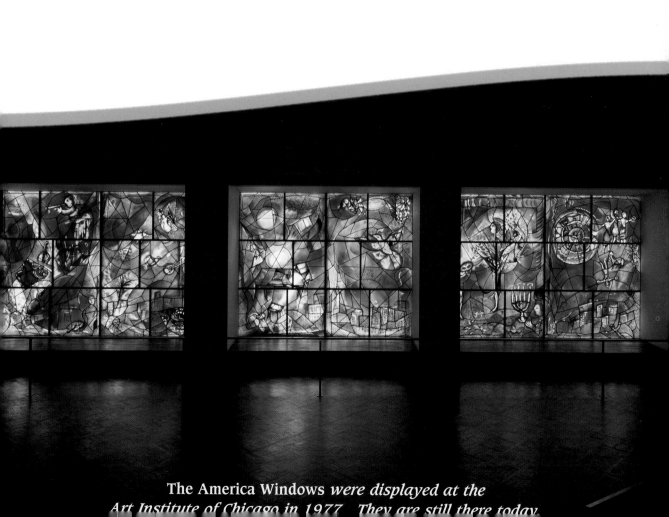

The America Windows *were displayed at the Art Institute of Chicago in 1977. They are still there today.*

Glossary

communism - a social and economic system in which everything is owned by the government and given to the people as needed.

concentration camp - a death camp where many Jews were sent during World War II.

critic - a professional who gives his or her opinion on art or performances.

criticize - to find fault with something.

geometry - a branch of mathematics that deals with shapes, lines, and angles.

Hebrew - the ancient language of the Jewish people.

rabbi - a leader or teacher in the Jewish religion.

Russian Revolution - two uprisings in 1917, one in March and one in October, during which the czar of Russia was overthrown and a communist government took over.

World War I - from 1914 to 1918, fought in Europe. Great Britain, France, Russia, the United States, and their allies were on one side. Germany, Austria-Hungary, and their allies were on the other side.

World War II - from 1939 to 1945, fought in Europe, Asia, and Africa. Great Britain, France, the United States, the Soviet Union, and their allies were on one side. Germany, Italy, Japan, and their allies were on the other side.

Saying It

Ambroise Vollard - AHN-BRWAWZ VAW-LAHR
Dvina - dvee-NAH
Hasidic - hah-SIH-dik
heder - KAY-duhr
Marc Chagall - MAHRK SHAH-GAHL
Nikolay Gogol - nyik-uh-LEYE GAW-guhl
Salon d'Automne - sah-LOHN doh-TUHM
Igor Stravinsky - EE-guhr struh-VYEEN-skeye
Vitebsk - VEE-tipsk

Web Sites

To learn more about Marc Chagall, visit ABDO Publishing Company on the World Wide Web at **www.abdopub.com**. Web sites about Chagall are featured on our Book Links page. These links are routinely monitored and updated to provide the most current information available.

Index